THE OLD RICKETY HOUSE

by Dilys Owen

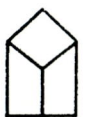

CRYSTAL CLEAR PUBLICATIONS Ltd.
LONDON

It was a quiet summer day without a breath of wind in the air. Behind the tool shed, Turbo and his friends, Kipper the Cat and Bones the Dog were having a competition to see who could hold their breath the longest. Nobody said a word.

Turbo pretended to see something in the sky. "What?" said Bones and Kipper, forgetting to hold their breath. "I won!" said Turbo. "Cheat!" said

the others.

"Let's explore the tool shed," he said. This was not a good idea.

Choose the Danger Spot which says why.

It was ever so dark in the shed and Turbo couldn't see a thing. He trod on a rake which hit him with a smack right on his chin.

Turbo fell back against the wall of the shed and saws with great big sharp teeth fell down all around him and cut him on his arms and legs.

Turbo came out of the shed scared stiff, and covered with cobwebs. "It's haunted," he jabbered. "A horrible monster cut my arm."

"Don't be silly," said Kipper, "Houses are haunted, not tool sheds." "I had a kennel once that was haunted," said Bones.

"I know," said Turbo, "let's play ghosts and see who can be the most scary. We'll all dress up and haunt each other. I bet I can frighten you more than you can frighten me," he boasted. They all went indoors to find some frightening costumes.

Later, the ghosts of Bones and the ghost of Kipper appeared wearing old white sheets. "Oooah!" they wailed and looked around for the ghost of Turbo.

Meanwhile, the ghost of Turbo was putting a plastic bag over his head, which was very dangerous.
Choose the Danger Spot that says why.

The ghosts of Bones and Kipper took it in turns to frighten each other. They were so frightened their knees knocked together.

The ghost of Turbo appeared. He was really frightening. He could not breathe with the plastic bag over his head.

Luckily his friends pulled off the bag just in time.
 Turbo decided that it would be safer to search for a real ghost instead of pretending to be one.
 "I know an old rickety house. It's bound to have a ghost," said Kipper.

They set off down a country lane towards the woods to find the old rickety house. They were all very excited. They held hands tightly because they had never seen a ghost before and didn't know how frightened they might be.

After a little while they came to a stream with a bridge across it. "Let's cross over by the bridge," said Bones and Kipper.

"It's more fun to jump across the stones," said Turbo. It was also more dangerous. Choose the Danger Spot which says why.

WATER CAN DROWN YOU

Suddenly, Turbo slipped on the wet stones, lost his balance and hit his head as he fell in the water.

He would have drowned but Kipper and Bones were quick to drag him onto the bank. "You are a silly tortoise," scolded Kipper and Bones.

At last they reached the old rickety house. It was very creepy. Bones said Kipper should go in because cats can see in the dark. Kipper said Bones should go in because dogs have a good sense of smell. In the end they decided Turbo should go and hide in his shell if the ghost wasn't friendly.

Turbo looked at the sign on the gate. "Look, there must be a ghost here," he said, "because the sign says DANGER".

But the sign said danger, because it was not safe for Turbo to go in.
Choose the Danger Spot which says why.

Inside the house it was dark and spooky. Suddenly, there was a ghostly creak and the floorboards broke.

Turbo crashed into the cellar and piles of rubble fell on top of him.

An ambulance arrived for Turbo.

When Turbo woke up he was in Hospital with lots of people dressed in white who reminded him of ghosts. Turbo would never forget his accident in the rickety house — neither will you. Remember Turbo's Danger Spots and play safely.